Mc Graw Hill Education

Cover and Title Page: Nathan Love

www.mheonline.com/readingwonders

Copyright © 2016 McGraw-Hill Education

All rights reserved. No part of this publication may be reproduced or distributed in any form or by any means, or stored in a database or retrieval system, without the prior written consent of McGraw-Hill Education, including, but not limited to, network storage or transmission or broadcast for distance learning.

Send all inquiries to:
McGraw-Hill Education
2 Penn Plaza
New York, NY 10121

ISBN: 978-0-02-130756-2
MHID: 0-02-130756-3

Printed in the United States of America

9 10 LMN 23

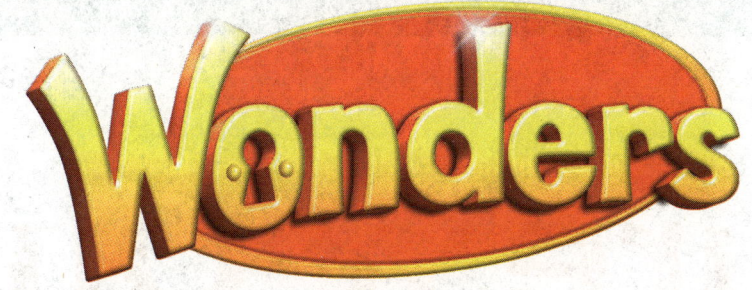

ELD
Companion Worktext

Program Authors

Diane August

Jana Echevarria

Josefina V. Tinajero

Unit 2

Figure It Out

The Big Idea
What does it take to solve a problem? 2

Week 1 • Cooperation   4

More Vocabulary 6
Shared Read   Anansi Learns a Lesson   Genre • Folktale 8
Respond to the Text 14
Write to Sources 16

Week 2 • Immigration   18

More Vocabulary 20
Shared Read   Sailing to America   Genre • Historical Fiction 22
Respond to the Text 28
Write to Sources 30

Week 3 • Government 32

More Vocabulary 34
Shared Read Every Vote Counts Genre • Expository Text 36
Respond to the Text 42
Write to Sources 44

Week 4 • Survival 46

More Vocabulary 48
Shared Read Kids to the Rescue! Genre • Expository Text 50
Respond to the Text 56
Write to Sources 58

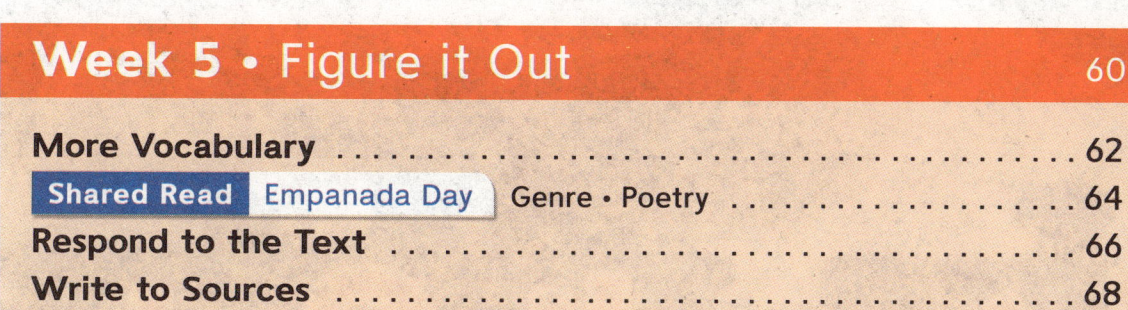

Week 5 • Figure it Out 60

More Vocabulary 62
Shared Read Empanada Day Genre • Poetry 64
Respond to the Text 66
Write to Sources 68

Unit 2

Figure It Out

The Big Idea

What does it take to solve a problem?

TALK ABOUT IT

Weekly Concept Cooperation

? Essential Question
Why is working together a good way to solve a problem?

>> *Go Digital*

 **What are these friends doing? Why is it a good way to solve a problem? Write the words in the web.**

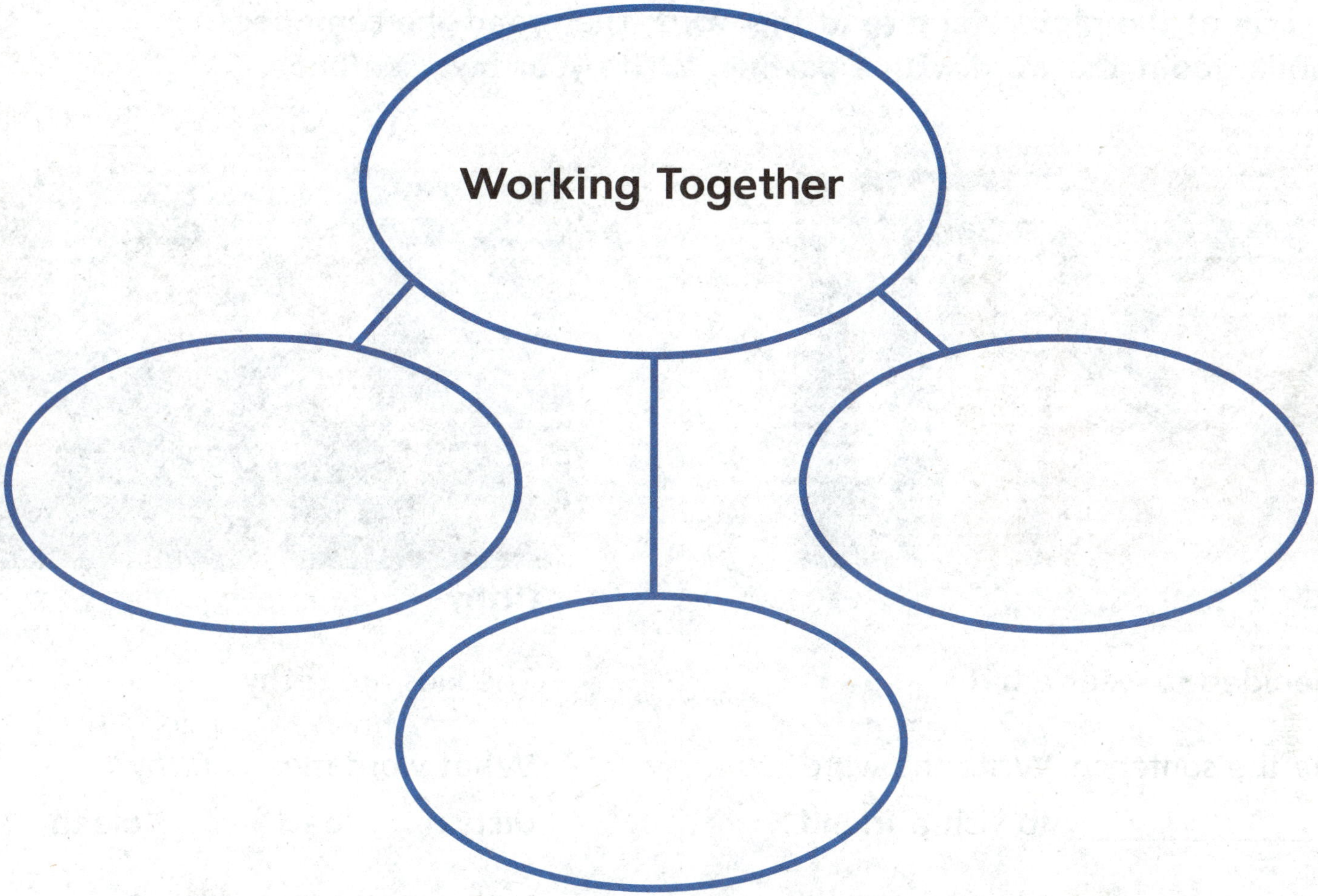

Working Together

Talk about how these friends are solving a problem. Use the words from the web. You can say:

These friends are _____.

Working together makes a job _____

_____.

More Vocabulary

 Look at the picture and read the word. Then read the sentences. Talk about the word with a partner. Write your own sentence.

decided

Emma **decided** to wear a hat.

Complete the sentence. Write the word.
We _____ to visit a friend.

What show did you decide to see?

I decided to see _____

_____.

filthy

The kids are **filthy**.

What word means *filthy*?
dirty   **bad**   **clean**

Why are the kids filthy?

The kids are filthy because they _____

_____.

6

Words and Phrases: Idioms with *help*

help yourself = take what you want

Can I have an apple?

Yes. You can **help yourself**.

need your help = want you to do something

What do you want?

I **need your help** to clean the dishes.

Talk with a partner. Look at the pictures. Read the sentences. Circle the words that complete each sentence.

You can _____
         help yourself   need your help
to the popcorn.

We _____
    help yourself   need your help
to rake the leaves.

Text Evidence

1 Talk About It

Look at the picture. Read the title. Discuss what you see. Use these words.

spider   banana   turtle   lesson

Write about what you see.

The story is about _____

_____

_____.

What does the title tell you?

A spider named Anansi will

_____.

Who do you think might teach Anansi a lesson?

I think _____ might teach Anansi a lesson.

Take notes as you read the text.

Shared Read — Genre • Folktale

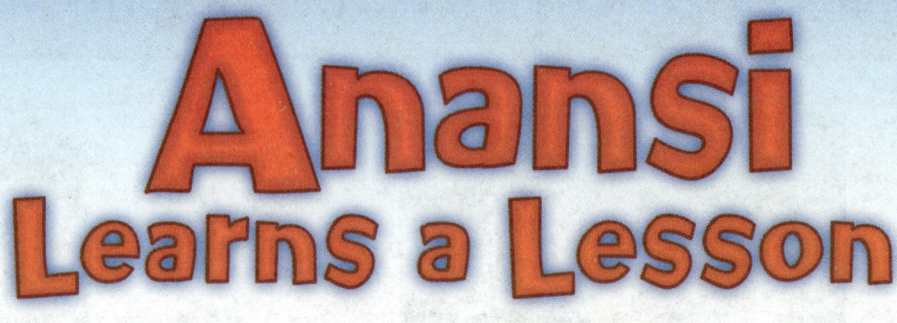

Anansi Learns a Lesson

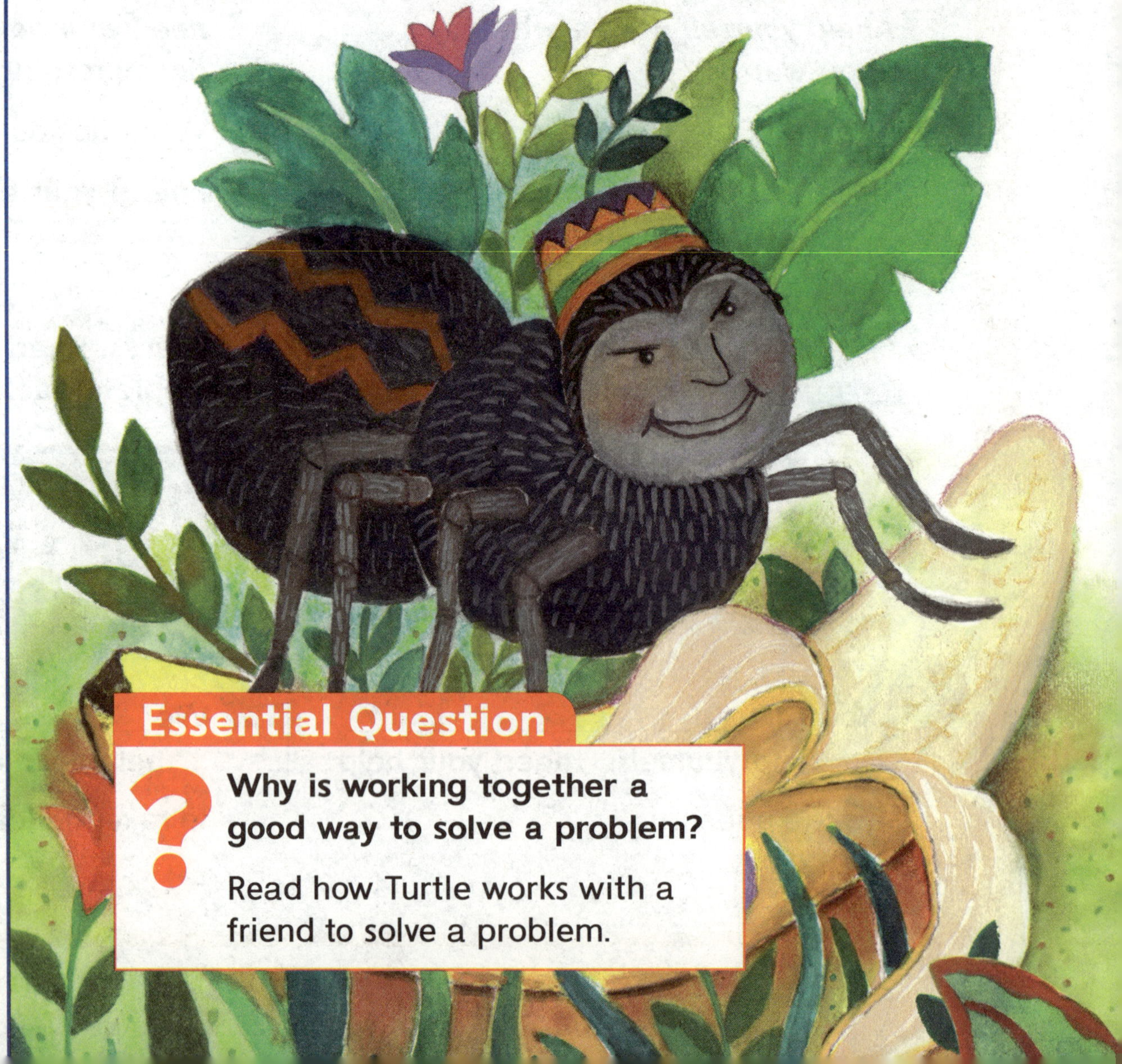

Essential Question

? Why is working together a good way to solve a problem?

Read how Turtle works with a friend to solve a problem.

Anansi the Spider was eating his lunch. Then Turtle came to visit Anansi. Turtle was a friend.

"Those bananas look good," said Turtle. "I am very hungry."

Anansi did not want to share his bananas. He was hungry. So Anansi **decided** to trick Turtle.

Anansi made a **sly** grin. "Help yourself," he said.

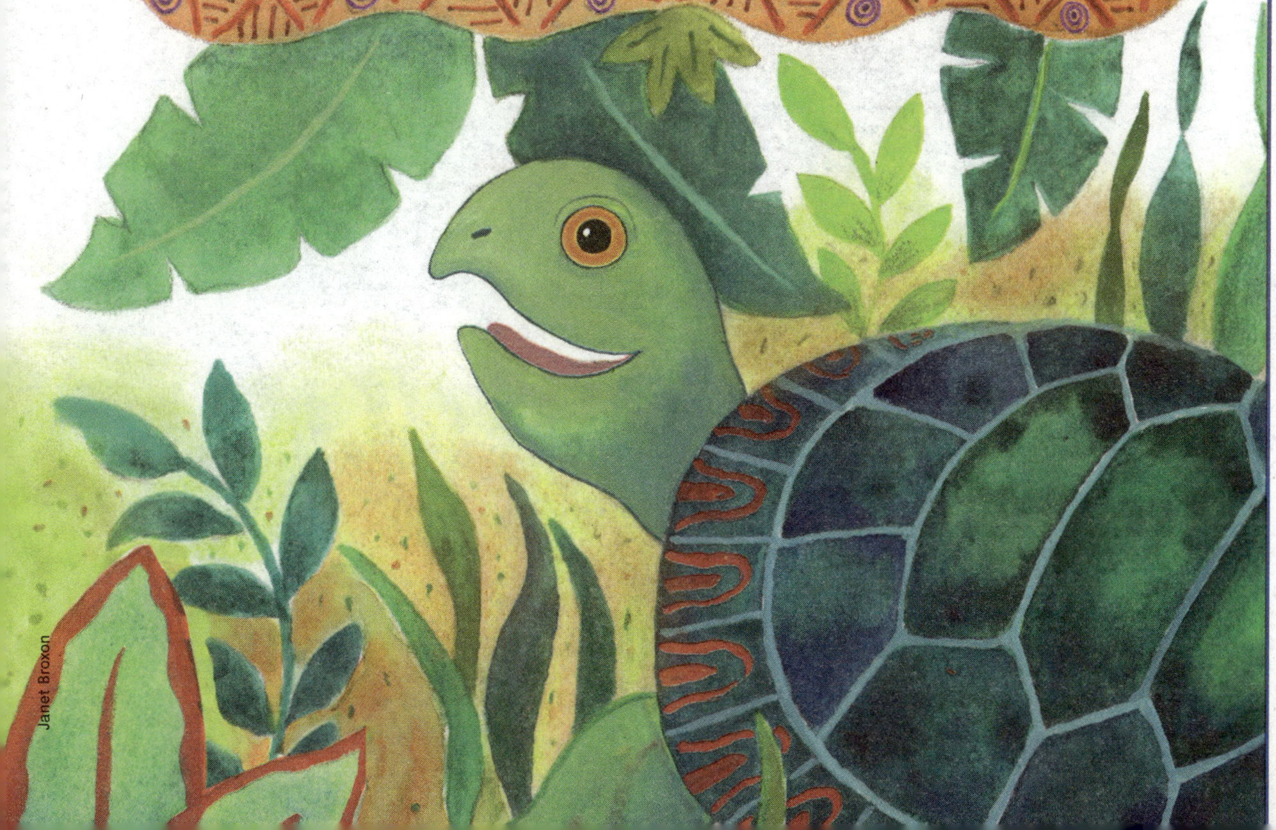

Text Evidence

1 Sentence Structure
Look at the first sentence in the first paragraph. Who is the sentence about? Circle the subject. Underline what the subject is doing.

2 Specific Vocabulary
Look at the word *sly*. Someone who is sly is able to fool others. What word in the third paragraph is a clue to the meaning of *sly*? Circle the word.

What does Anansi say after he makes a sly grin?

Anansi says _____.

3 Talk About It
Is Anansi a good friend to Turtle? Why or why not?

Write reasons for your answer.

_____

_____

Text Evidence

1. Sentence Structure ACT

Look at the second sentence in the second paragraph. Circle the pronoun. What word does the pronoun refer to?

2. Specific Vocabulary ACT

Look at the third paragraph. The word *spoil* shows when food goes bad. What can spoil in the story?

_____

3. Talk About It

Think about what you have read so far. Discuss why Turtle does not eat any bananas. What does Anansi do with the bananas?

When Turtle is gone, Anansi _____.

Turtle reached for the food. "Please wash your hands," said Anansi. So Turtle went to wash his hands.

Then Turtle came back, and part of the bananas were gone. Anansi ate them.

"I did not want them to **spoil**," said Anansi.

Turtle made another attempt to eat. Anansi stopped him again.

"Please wash your hands," he said.

Turtle knew his hands were clean. But Anansi thought they were **filthy**. Turtle was too shy to say no. When Turtle returned, the bananas were gone.

"I tricked you," said Anansi. "Ha, ha, ha."

Turtle was mad. He decided to teach Anansi a lesson. "Anansi, please come to my house for dinner. It is at the bottom of the lake," said Turtle.

Anansi said yes. He loved **free** food.

Turtle wanted to trick Anansi, but Turtle needed help. So Turtle found Fish in the lake.

"Fish, I need your help," Turtle said. "Together we will trick Anansi."

Fish was happy to help. So the two friends worked together and made a plan.

Text Evidence

❶ Specific Vocabulary

Look at the second paragraph. *Free* describes something that does not cost money. Why do you think Anansi loves free food?

Anansi loves free food because

_____.

❷ Sentence Structure

Reread the first sentence in the third paragraph. Circle the word that connects Turtle's two actions. Underline the actions.

❸ Comprehension
Theme

Reread the last paragraph. Underline the detail that tells what Fish and Turtle do together.

Text Evidence

1 Specific Vocabulary

The word *float* means "to stay on top of water." Look at the fourth paragraph. What word means the opposite of *float*? Write the word.

_____

2 Sentence Structure

Look at the first sentence in the fifth paragraph. What does Anansi do? Circle the word that connects Anansi's two actions. Underline the two actions.

3 Talk About It

How do stones help Anansi go to Turtle's house?

The stones help Anansi _____

_____.

Fish met Anansi at the lake the next day. "We will swim to Turtle's house together," said Fish.

Anansi jumped into the water. But he was not a good swimmer. He was also very light.

"How will I swim down to Turtle's house?" he cried.

"Grab some heavy stones. You will sink. You will not **float**," Fish said.

Anansi picked up two big stones and jumped into the lake. He sank to Turtle's house. Fish swam beside Anansi. Then Anansi saw a feast of berries at Turtle's house.

"Welcome, Anansi!" said Turtle. "Drop those stones. Help yourself."

Anansi dropped the stones. Then he rocketed to the top of the lake. "Fish and Turtle tricked me," he cried.

Turtle and Fish laughed.

"We worked together, and we taught Anansi a lesson," said Turtle.

"And we solved a problem," said Fish.

"Let's eat!"

Make Connections

? Tell how Turtle and Fish work together to trick Anansi. **ESSENTIAL QUESTION**

When did you and a friend solve a problem? Why was it easier to work together? **TEXT TO SELF**

Text Evidence

❶ Sentence Structure ACT

Look at the second paragraph. Who does the word *he* refer to? Write the name.

_____

❷ Comprehension
Theme

Reread the fourth and fifth paragraphs. Fish and Turtle tell the theme of the story. Circle the two sentences that tell the theme.

❸ Talk About It

How do Turtle and Fish trick Anansi?

Turtle and Fish _____

_____.

Respond to the Text

 **Partner Discussion** Work with a partner. Read the questions about "Anansi Learns a Lesson." Show where you found text evidence. Write the page numbers. Then discuss what you learned.

What problem does Turtle have?

I read that Turtle wants _____. Page(s): _____

Anansi tricks Turtle by _____. Page(s): _____

Turtle decides to teach Anansi _____. Page(s): _____

Text Evidence

How do Turtle and Fish work together?

Turtle asks Anansi _____. Page(s): _____

Turtle and Fish make _____. Page(s): _____

After Anansi drops the stones, he _____. Page(s): _____

Text Evidence

 **Group Discussion** Present your answers to the group. Cite text evidence for your ideas. Listen to and discuss the group's opinions.

Write Work with a partner. Look at your notes about "Anansi Learns a Lesson." Write your answer to the Essential Question. Use text evidence to support your answer. Use vocabulary words in your writing.

> **How do Turtle and Fish work together to teach Anansi a lesson?**
>
> Turtle wants to teach _____ a lesson because _____
>
> _____.
>
> Turtle and Fish make a plan to _____.
>
> Turtle and Fish trick Anansi by _____
>
> _____.

Share Writing Present your writing to the class. Discuss their opinions. Talk about their ideas. Explain why you agree or disagree with their ideas. You can say:

I agree with _____.

I do not agree because _____.

Write to Sources

Luis

Take Notes About the Text I took notes on about the story on the chart. I used the notes to respond to the prompt: *Add a paragraph to the end of the story. Have Fish and Turtle tell Anansi why they tricked him.*

pages 8–13

Anansi will not share his bananas.

↓

Anansi decides to trick Turtle.

↓

Anansi tells Turtle to wash his hands.

↓

Anansi eats all the bananas.

Write About the Text My descriptive paragraph tells how Turtle and Fish tell Anansi why they tricked him.

Student Model: *Narrative Text*

"Why did you trick me?" Anansi asked.

Turtle said, "I was mad. You tricked me."

Fish said, "It is not nice to trick people."

Turtle said, "You made me wash my hands. Then you ate the bananas."

Fish said, "We wanted to teach you a lesson."

Anansi was sad.

TALK ABOUT IT

Text Evidence

Draw a box around the ideas that come from the chart.

Grammar

Circle a past-tense verb in the second paragraph. Tell if it describes an action, or helps describe what someone said or how someone feels.

Connect Ideas

Draw an arrow next to the second paragraph. How can you use the word *because* to connect the ideas?

Your Turn

Add a paragraph to the end of the story. Tell what Anansi does next.

≫ *Go Digital*
Write your response online. Use your editing checklist.

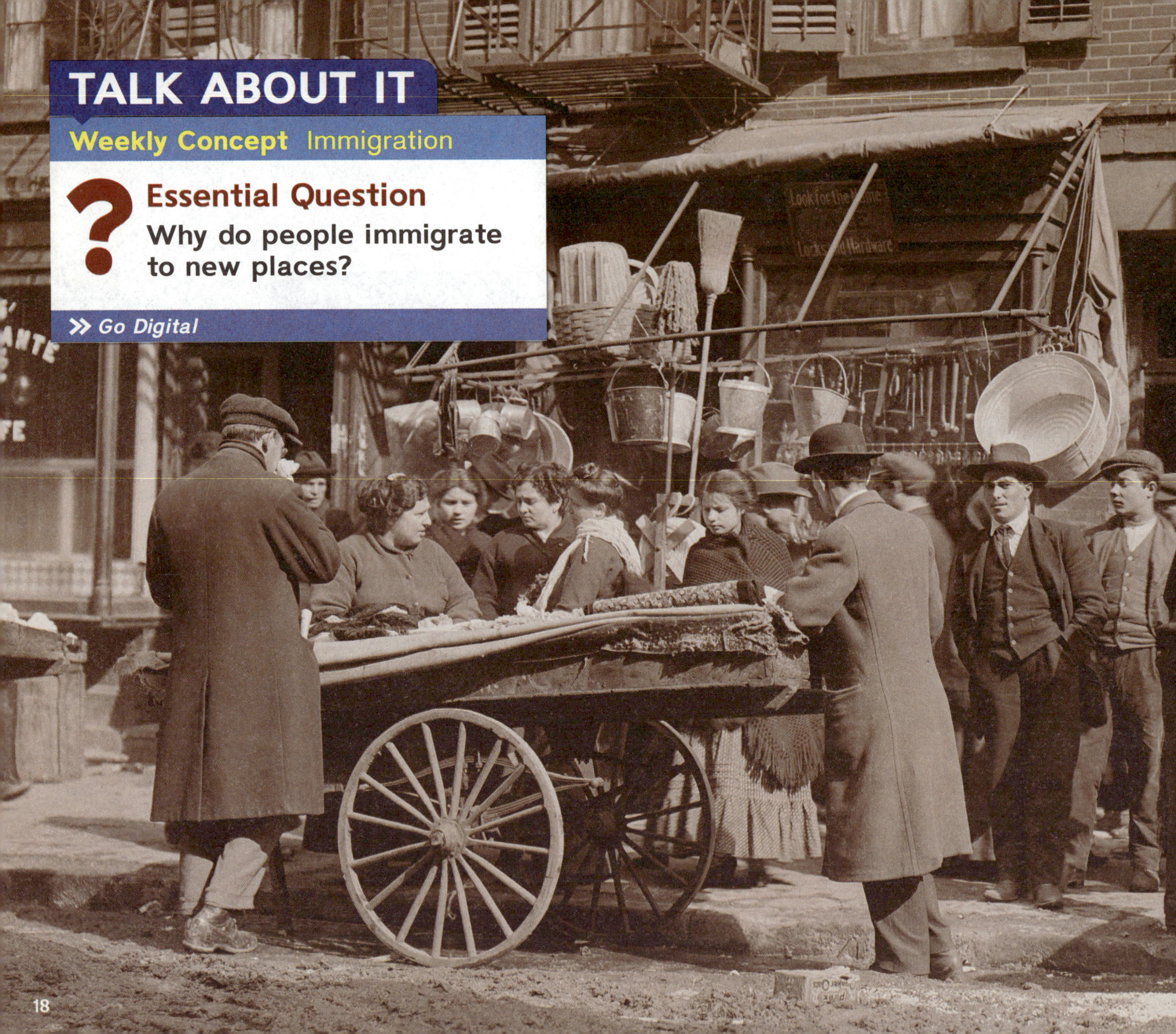

TALK ABOUT IT

Weekly Concept Immigration

? Essential Question
Why do people immigrate to new places?

>> Go Digital

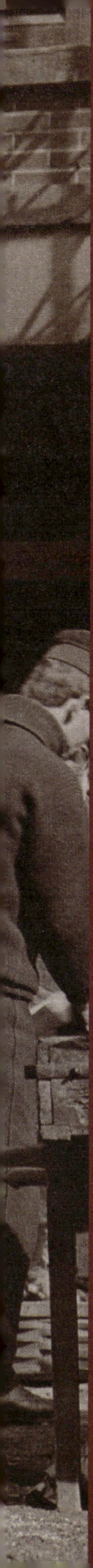

 **Immigrants are people who move to a new place. Why do immigrants move to new places? Write the words in the web.**

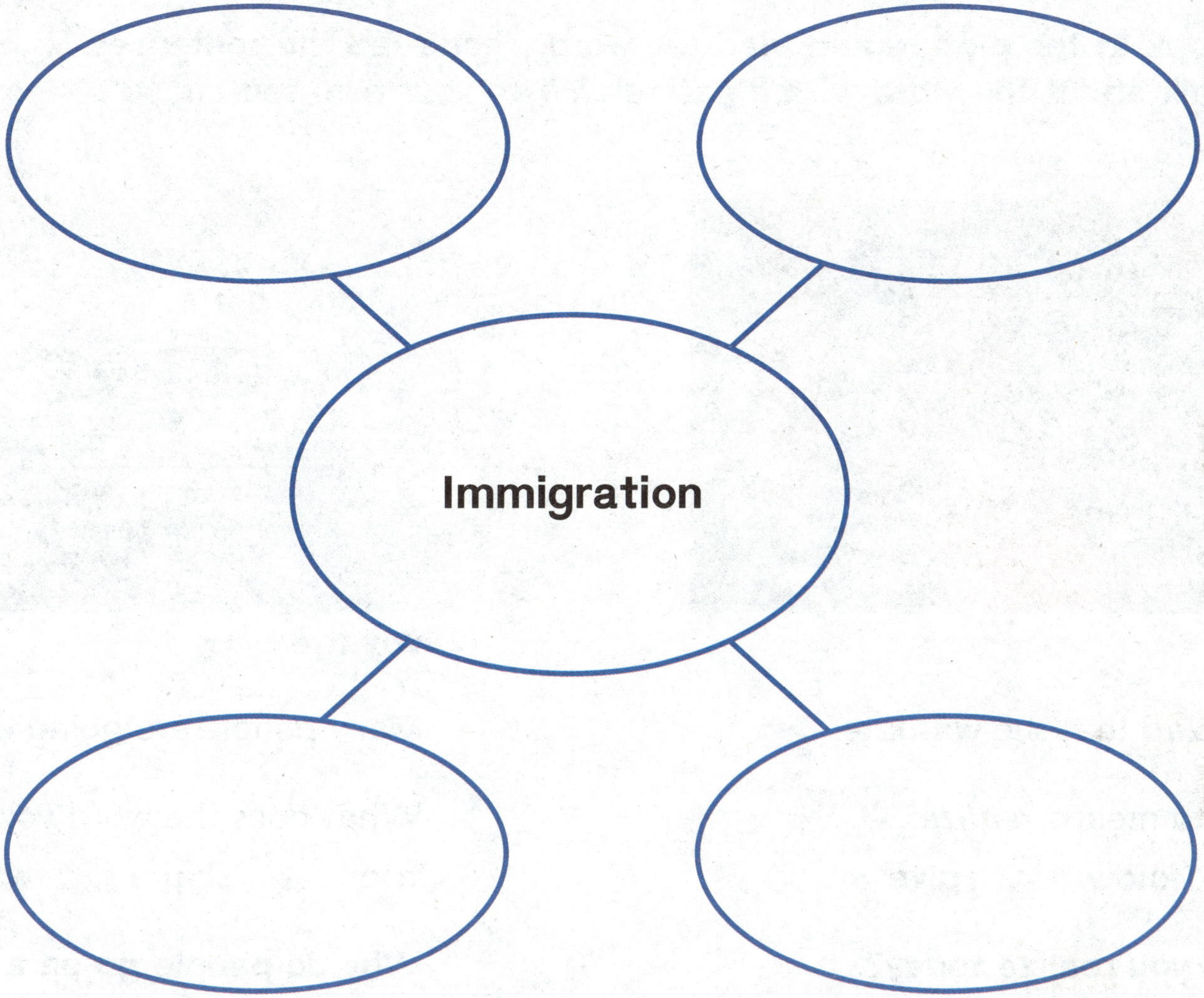

Immigration

Talk about why these people immigrated. Use the words from the web. You can say:

Many immigrants move _____.

Immigrants want a _____.

More Vocabulary

Look at the picture and read the word. Then read the sentences. Talk about the word with a partner. Write your own sentence.

realize

May **realized** that she was late.

What word means *realize*?
like   know   give

What did you realize today?

I realized that _____
_____
_____.

voyage

Many people are going on a **voyage**.

What does the word *voyage* mean?
trip   ship   wave

Why do people go on a voyage?

People go on a voyage _____
_____
_____.

Words and Phrases: Contractions *doesn't* and *don't*

The contraction *doesn't* means *does not*.

The boy does not like the sound.

The boy **doesn't** like the sound.

The contraction *don't* means *do not*.

The girls do not like the rain.

The girls **don't** like the rain.

Talk with a partner. Look at the pictures. Read the sentences. Write the word that completes the sentence.

The bike _____ work.
doesn't   don't

The boys _____ like the water.
doesn't   don't

Text Evidence

Shared Read | Genre • Historical Fiction

1 Talk About It

Look at the picture. Read the title. Discuss what you see. Use these words.

brother   photographs   sister

Write about what you see.

The story is about _____

_____.

What are the children doing?

The brother and sister are

_____

_____.

When does the story happen?

The story happens _____

_____.

Take notes as you read the text.

SAILING TO AMERICA

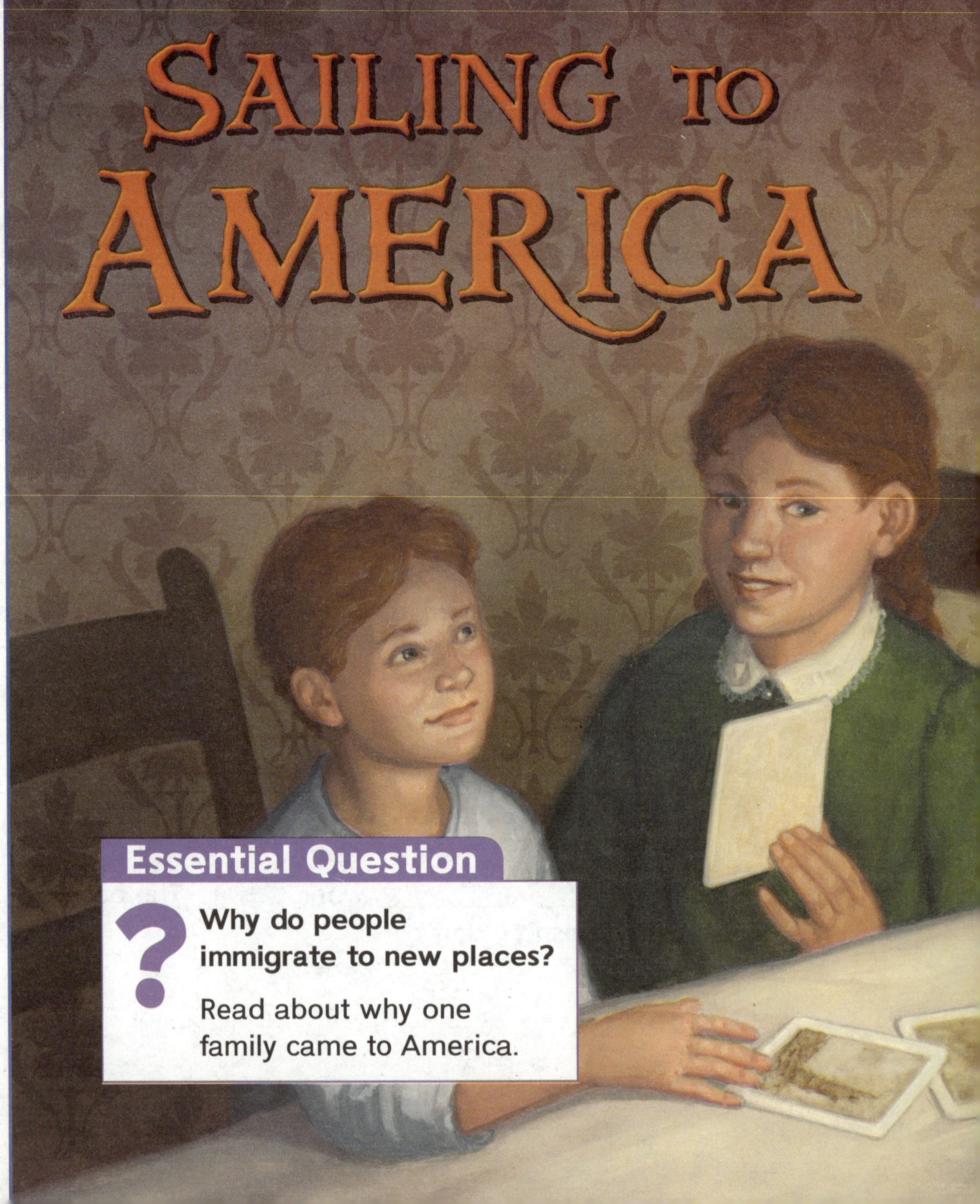

Essential Question

? Why do people immigrate to new places?

Read about why one family came to America.

Nora woke up early. It was March, 1895. Da was leaving for America today. Uncle Sean immigrated there last year. Now Da was going to join him. It was Mama and Da's **dream** to live in America.

Nora lit a lamp and sat at the table. Her brother, Danny, sat down beside her.

Danny said, "I am sad."

"I am sad, too," said Nora. "But Da will find work in America. Then we can go there, too. Now, look at these photographs. Uncle Sean sent them. Doesn't America look great?"

Text Evidence

1 Specific Vocabulary

Look at the last sentence of the first paragraph. Circle the word *dream*. Here, *dream* is another word for *hope*. What is Mama and Da's dream?

Mama and Da hope to _____
_____.

2 Sentence Structure

Look at the fourth paragraph. Who does the pronoun *we* refer to? Write the names.

_____

3 Talk About It

Why is Da going to America?

Da is going to America because
_____.

Text Evidence

1 Sentence Structure

Look at the first paragraph. Circle the punctuation marks. Who is speaking? Write the name.

_____

2 Specific Vocabulary

Reread the third paragraph. *Cheer up* means "to not feel sad." Underline the sentence that tells why Nora and Danny should cheer up.

3 Talk About It

Why does Nora want to go to America?

Nora thinks that _____

_____

"I don't want to leave Ireland," Danny cried. "We will not have friends in America. We will be far away from our friends here."

"We will have a better life," Nora said. "America will be the land of our dreams."

Then Da came into the room. "**Cheer up**! You will join me soon."

A year later, Da had enough money. He asked Mama, Danny, and Nora to come to America. The family packed their bags. Then they got on a crowded steamship and began their **voyage**.

The trip was **rough**. The air inside the steamship smelled like a dirty sock. The ship moved up and down. The waves were as big as mountains. Many people were sick. But Nora and Danny were fine.

Nora daydreamed every day. She reread Da's letters. In her dreams, she saw Da on a crowded street. He was smiling.

Text Evidence

1 Sentence Structure

Reread the last sentence in the first paragraph. Circle the words *they* and *their*. Who do *they* and *their* refer to? Underline the names.

2 Specific Vocabulary

Look at the word *rough*. Something that is rough is not easy. What sentences help you understand the meaning of *rough*? Underline the sentences.

COLLABORATE

3 Talk About It

What clues show that Nora wants to see Da?

Nora wants to _____

because _____

_____.

Text Evidence

1 Specific Vocabulary

Something that is smooth does not have bumps. Read the first paragraph. What is smooth? Write the word.

_____

2 Sentence Structure

Reread the second paragraph. What punctuation mark shows excitement? Circle it. Why is the crowd excited?

The crowd is excited because

_____.

3 Talk About It

How do the travelers on the boat feel about America?

The travelers feel _____

because _____.

Nora woke up one morning and **realized** something was different. The ocean was as **smooth** as glass. Nora, Danny, and Mama walked to the deck of the boat. The family sat together and watched the snow begin to fall.

Then someone shouted, "There is Lady Liberty!" The ship passed the large statue.

"We are in America!" the travelers cheered. Soon, everyone was singing and dancing.

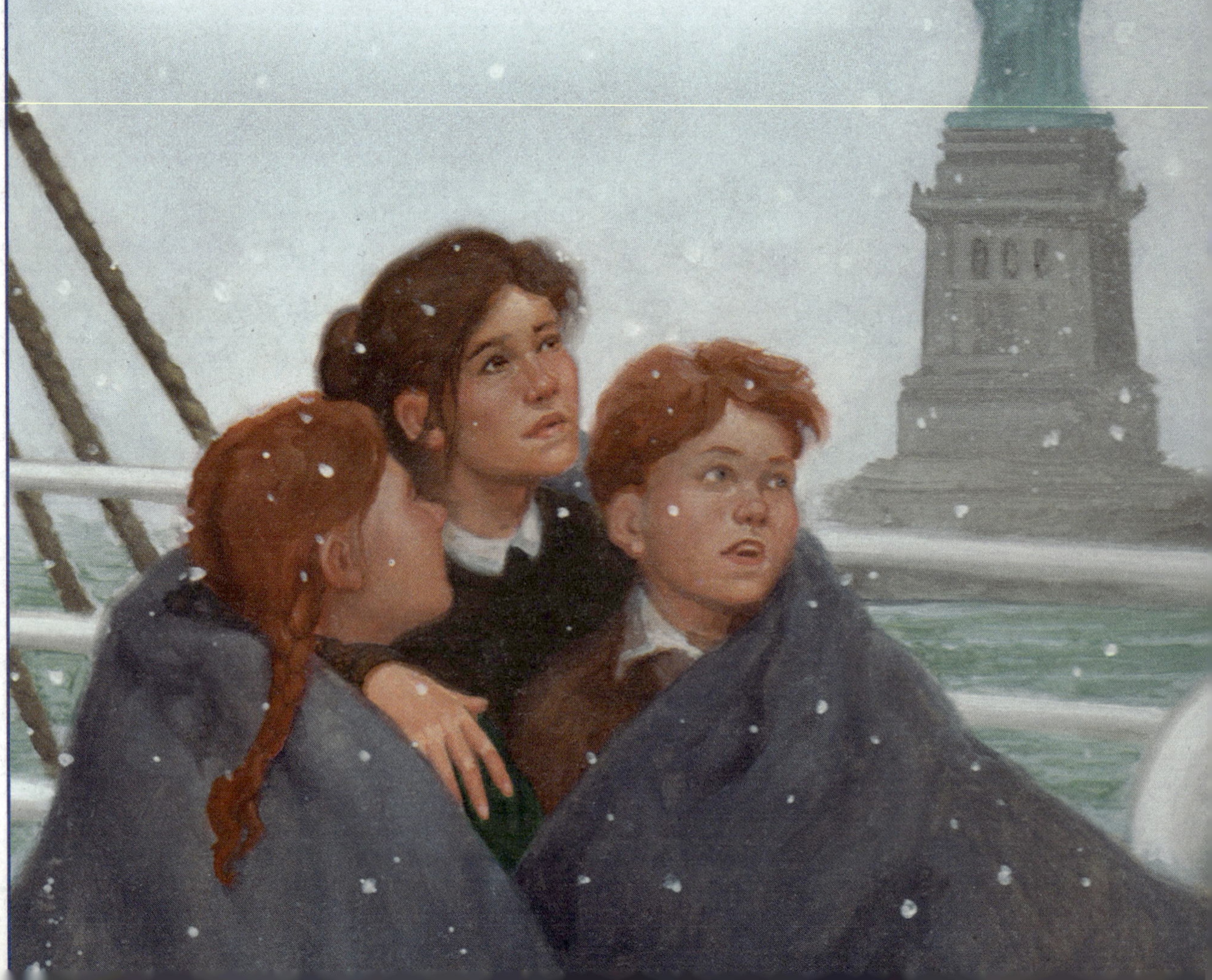

Then the travelers went to Ellis Island. Doctors there inspected the travelers. Sick people could not stay in America. Mama answered many questions. Nora felt afraid. This was the family's only chance to stay in America. They had to pass.

Nora, Danny, and Mama waited for a few hours. Then they learned the good news. They were staying in America. Then they left the boat. Nora saw Da. He waved wildly and smiled. Nora waved, too. She thought, "Dreams do come true."

Make Connections

Why do Nora and her family immigrate to America? ESSENTIAL QUESTION

Did someone in your family move to a new place? How did they feel? TEXT TO SELF

Text Evidence

1 Sentence Structure ACT
Reread the first sentence in the second paragraph. How long does the family wait? Underline the words that tell you.

2 Talk About It
Why does Nora feel afraid on Ellis Island? Write your ideas.

Nora feels afraid because _____

_____.

3 Comprehension
Theme

Reread the last paragraph. Think about key details in the story. Which sentence tells the theme of the story? Underline the sentence.

Respond to the Text

 **Partner Discussion** Work with a partner. Read the questions about "Sailing to America." Show where you found text evidence. Write the page numbers. Then discuss what you learned.

Why do Nora and her family want to move to America?

Mama and Da's dream is _____. Page(s): _____

In the story, Nora thinks America is _____. Page(s): _____

Da asks his family _____ after he _____. Page(s): _____

How does the family feel when they come to America?

The passengers cheer when _____. Page(s): _____

Nora, Danny, and Mama are afraid because _____
_____. Page(s): _____

In the story, Nora sees Da and knows _____. Page(s): _____

 **Group Discussion** Present your answers to the group. Cite text evidence for your ideas. Listen to and discuss the group's opinions.

 **Write** Work with a partner. Look at your notes about "Sailing to America." Write your answer to the Essential Question. Use text evidence to support your answer. Use vocabulary words in your writing.

Why do Nora and her family want to immigrate to America?

Da goes to America because _____

_____.

Nora thinks America is _____ because _____

_____.

Nora, Danny, and Mama go to America because _____.

Nora sees Da in America and feels _____

_____.

Share Writing Present your writing to the class. Discuss their opinions. Talk about their ideas. Explain why you agree or disagree with their ideas. You can say:

I think your ideas are _____.

I do not agree with you because _____.

Write to Sources

Rachel

Take Notes About the Text I took notes about the story on this idea web to answer the question: *Was it a good idea for Nora and her family to come to America? Tell why or why not.*

pages 22–27

- I think it was a good idea.
  - It is Mama and Da's dream to live in America.
  - Da finds work.
  - Nora thinks they will have a better life.

Write About the Text I used notes from my idea web to write an opinion.

Student Model: *Opinion*

I think it was a good idea for Nora and her family to come to America on a steamship. Nora thinks they will have a better life. It is Mama's dream. It is Da's dream. Da finds work in America. I think that Nora's family makes the right choice.

TALK ABOUT IT

Text Evidence
Circle the first sentence. Which noun tells how Nora's family got to America?

Grammar
Underline the sentence about Da finding work. Which words tell where Da will find work?

Connect Ideas
Draw a box around the sentences about dreams. How can you combine the sentences?

Your Turn

Does the author do a good job of explaining why the family moves to America? Tell how you know.

>> *Go Digital*
Write your response online. Use your editing checklist.

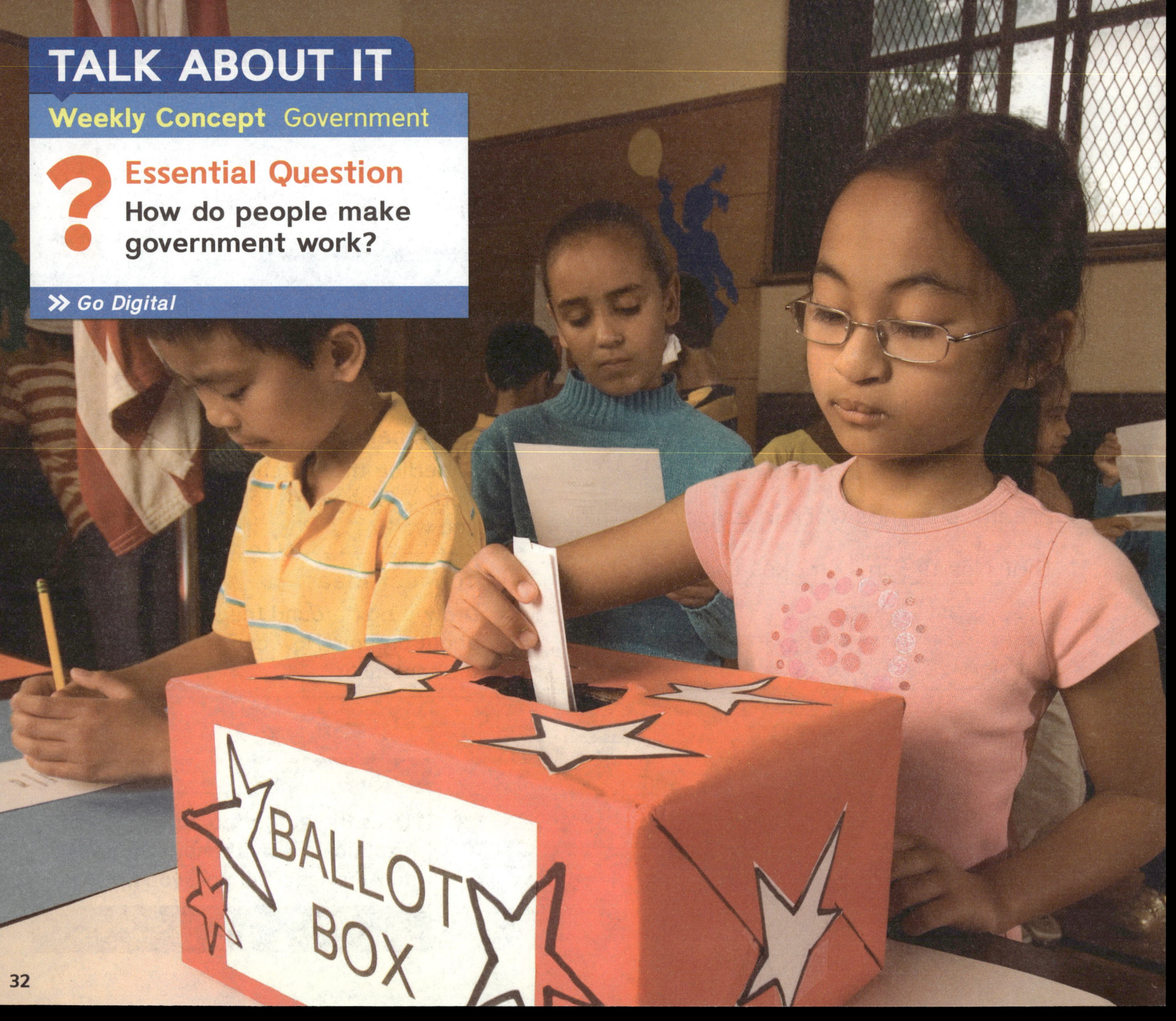

TALK ABOUT IT

Weekly Concept Government

? Essential Question
How do people make government work?

>> *Go Digital*

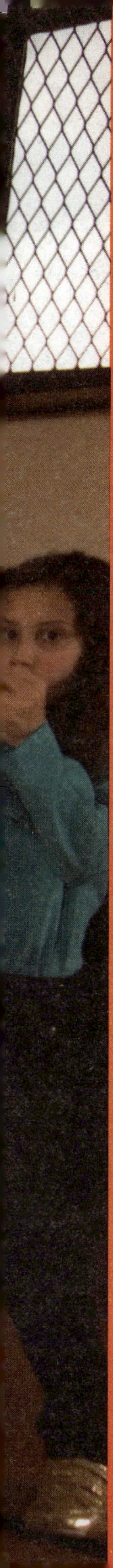

 **What are these kids doing? Why is it important to vote? Write the words in the web.**

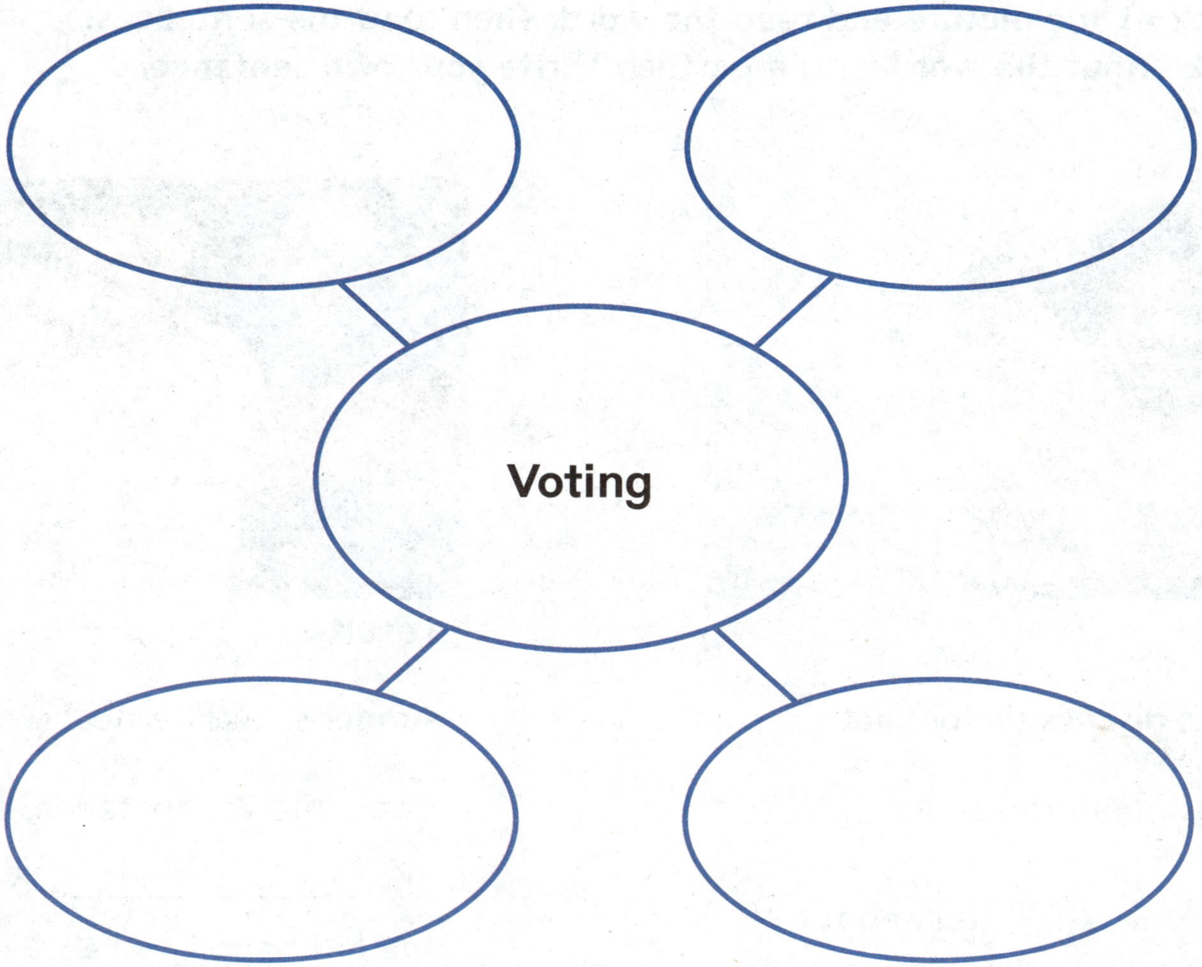

Voting

Talk about voting. Why is voting important? Use the words from the web. You can say:

Voting is important because _____

_____.

More Vocabulary

 Look at the picture and read the word. Then read the sentences. Talk about the word with a partner. Write your own sentence.

discuss

results

The students **discuss** the project.

What words mean the same as *discuss*?

run to   look at   talk about

What do you discuss with your class?

We discuss _____

_____

_____.

Amber shows her test **results**.

Complete the sentence. Write the word.

The _____ on the test make the girl happy.

When do you get good results?

I get good results after I _____

_____

_____.

Words and Phrases: Prefixes *un-* and *re-*

The prefix *un-* means "not."

Is the boy happy?

No. The boy is **un**happy.

The prefix *re-* means "again."

Will Pat use the bottle again?

Yes. Pat will **re**use the bottle.

 Talk with a partner. Look at the pictures. Read the sentences. Circle the meaning of the underlined word.

The street is <u>unclean</u>.
not clean   clean again

Rob <u>reties</u> his shoes.
does not tie   ties again

Text Evidence

Shared Read | Genre • Expository

1 Talk About It

Look at the picture. Read the title. Discuss what you see. Use these words.

class   counts   pet   vote

Write about what you see.

The text is about a _____

_____

_____.

What is the class voting for?

The class is voting for _____

_____

_____.

Take notes as you read the text.

Essential Question

? How do people make government work?

Read about a group that teaches kids the power of voting.

Every VOTE Counts!

Vote for the Class Pet

Have you voted? Maybe you voted to **choose** a class pet. Maybe you voted to choose a movie. Voting is important. It tells people what you think.

Long ago, our country's leaders wanted to know what people thought. The leaders wrote a plan for our government. The plan is called the Constitution. This plan gives people in the United States the right to vote.

Every year, people vote. They pick new leaders. People also vote for new laws. Voting gives people the power to choose.

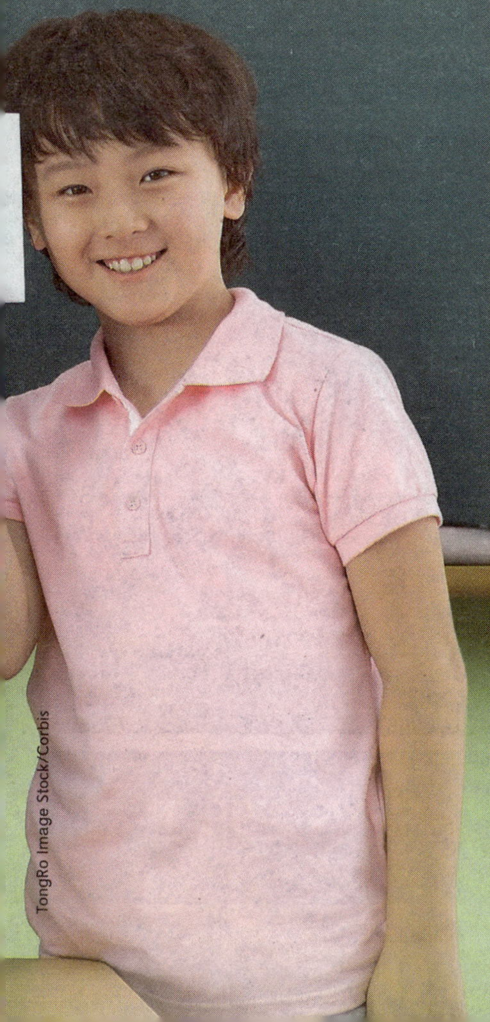

Text Evidence

1 Specific Vocabulary

The word *choose* means "to decide what you want." Read the last paragraph. Find a word in the sentence that means the same as *choose*. Circle the word.

2 Comprehension
Author's Point of View

Reread the first paragraph. How does the author feel about voting? Underline the sentence that tells you.

3 Talk About It

Why can people in the United States vote?

People can vote because _____

_____

_____

37

Text Evidence

1 Comprehension
Author's Point of View

Look at the first paragraph. How many people do not vote? Underline how the author feels about this fact.

2 Sentence Structure

Reread the third sentence of the second paragraph. Circle the connecting word *and*. What do the kids do?

Kids _____.

Kids _____.

3 Talk About It

How does Kids Voting USA help teachers and kids?

Kids Voting USA gives teachers

and kids _____

_____.

Teaching Kids to Vote

Many people do not vote. That is sad. Voting is hard for some people. They are unsure where to vote. They think voting takes too much time. Now, Kids Voting USA is getting more people to vote.

Kids Voting USA teaches kids about voting. The group gives teachers lessons to use. First, kids read stories and do fun activities. And they learn how to choose a good leader.

Election Day is here!

First we sign in.

Next, kids talk about voting with their families. They reread stories about candidates. Candidates are people. They want to be leaders. Families **discuss** the candidates' ideas. Then kids decide who to vote for.

Adults and kids vote on Election Day. Both adults and kids use **ballots** for voting. A ballot is a special form. First, kids mark their choices on the ballot. Then they put the ballot into a special box. Last, all the votes are counted. A winner is announced. So everyone knows the winner.

Then we mark a ballot.

Finally we vote!

Text Evidence

1 Sentence Structure ACT

Look at the fifth sentence in the first paragraph. Circle the possessive noun *candidates'*. What do the candidates have?

_____

2 Specific Vocabulary ACT

Look at the second paragraph. A *ballot* is a piece of paper you use to mark your vote. Write two things kids do with a ballot.

Kids _____ the

ballot. Then they _____.

3 Talk About It

How can kids learn about candidates?

Kids can talk with _____

_____.

Kids can reread _____.

39

Text Evidence

1 Sentence Structure

Read the first paragraph. Circle the punctuation mark for a question. Underline the sentences that answer that question.

2 Specific Vocabulary

When people *think for themselves*, they think without the help of others. Look at the third sentence. What can kids do to show they think for themselves?

Kids can think for themselves by

_____.

3 Talk About It

What is the author's opinion about kids voting?

The author thinks kids voting is

_____.

Vote Now

Kids Voting USA wants kids to vote when they are young. Why? Kids will learn how to **think for themselves**. They will learn how to share ideas. And when kids grow up, they will vote in real elections.

Kids your age will be old enough to vote in about ten years. They will elect great leaders and make laws. That is exciting!

Many schools hold elections. Elections teach kids how to vote.

This is a bar graph. It shows the **results** of a class election. Which pet was the *favorite*?

Make Connections

? How does voting give people the power to choose? ESSENTIAL QUESTION

Tell about a time when you voted. How did it make you feel? TEXT TO SELF

Text Evidence

1 **Specific Vocabulary**

Look at the question at the end of the paragraph. *Favorite* describes the most popular thing. What word does *favorite* describe in this question? Underline it.

2 **Talk About It**

What are the results of the election for a class pet? Discuss how the class voted.

The class decided _____

_____

_____.

41

Respond to the Text

 **Partner Discussion** Work with a partner. Read the questions about "Every Vote Counts!" Show where you found text evidence. Write the page numbers. Then discuss what you learned.

Why do people in our country vote?

In the text, our country's leaders wanted _____.

Voting is important because _____

_____.

I read that people vote for _____ and _____.

Text Evidence

Page(s): _____

Page(s): _____

Page(s): _____

How does Kids Voting USA teach kids to vote?

Kids Voting USA teaches _____.

In the text, kids and adults vote _____.

I read that Kids Voting USA wants _____.

Text Evidence

Page(s): _____

Page(s): _____

Page(s): _____

 **Group Discussion** Present your answers to the group. Cite text evidence for your ideas. Listen to and discuss the group's opinions.

42

Write Work with a partner. Look at your notes about "Every Vote Counts!" Write your answer to the Essential Question. Use text evidence to support your answer. Use vocabulary words in your writing.

> **How does voting help government work?**
>
> Voting began because _____ wanted to know _____
>
> _____.
>
> Now people vote for _____ and _____.
>
> Kids Voting USA teaches kids _____
>
> _____.
>
> On Election Day, kids and adults _____.

Share Writing Present your writing to the class. Discuss their opinions. Talk about their ideas. Explain why you agree or disagree with their ideas. You can say:

I agree with _____.

That's a good idea, but _____.

Write to Sources

Marlon

Take Notes About the Text I took notes about the text. I will use the notes to answer the question: *Do you think the author shows why people should vote? Think about the reasons the author gives.*

pages 36–41

- Voting gives people the power to choose.
- **The author shows why people should vote.**
- The author says voting tells people what you think.
- Voting helps kids think for themselves.

Write About the Text I used notes from my idea web to write an opinion.

Student Model: *Opinion*

    I think the author shows why people should vote. The author gives reasons and explains why. The author says voting tells people what you think. Voting gives people the power to choose. Voting helps kids think for themselves. These are good reasons to vote!

TALK ABOUT IT

Text Evidence
Circle the third sentence. Does this sentence support the author's opinion that people should vote? Why or why not?

Grammar
Draw a box around the last sentence. What adjective adds information about the noun *reasons*?

Connect Ideas
Circle things the author does in sentence two. What word connects these ideas?

Your Turn

Do you agree or disagree with the author's ideas on voting? Use text evidence in your answer.

>> *Go Digital*
Write your response online. Use your editing checklist.

TALK ABOUT IT

Weekly Concept Survival

? Essential Question
How can people help animals survive?

>> *Go Digital*

 **These manatees are threatened animals. How can we help threatened animals survive? Write the words in the web.**

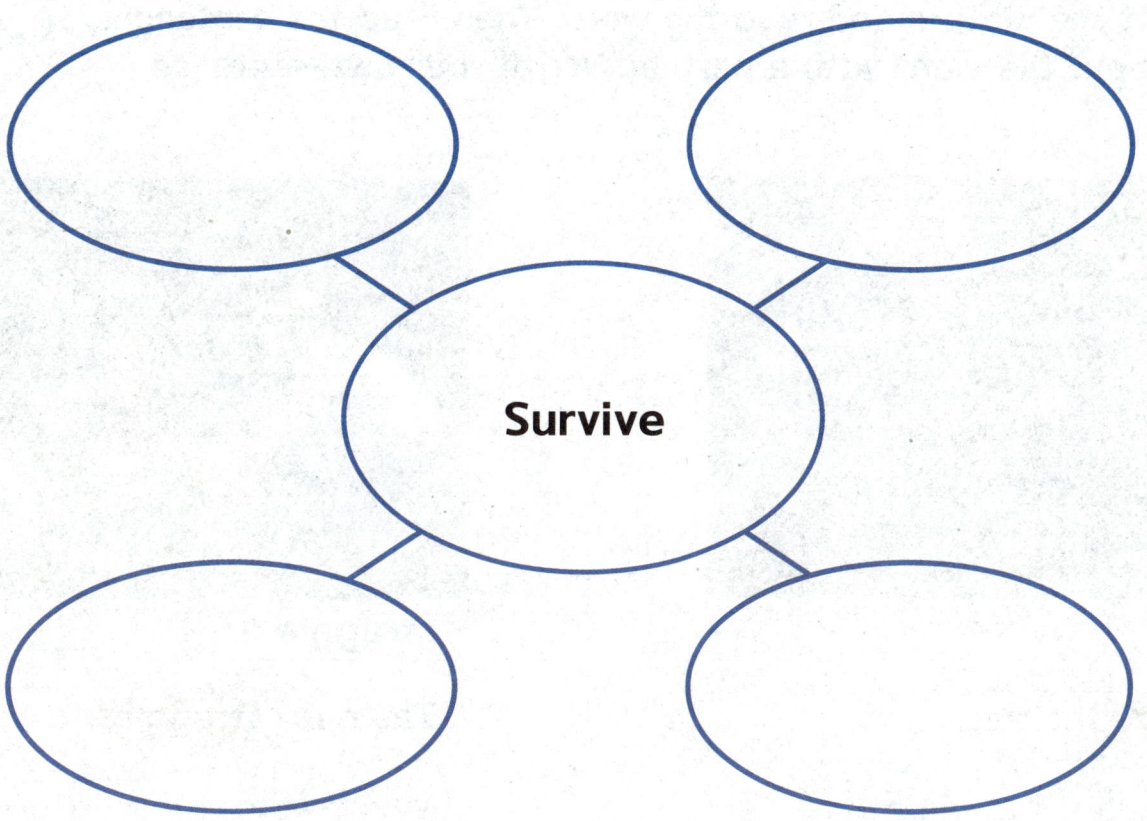

Talk about what animals need. Tell how people can help animals. Use the words from the web. You can say:

Animals need _____

_____ to survive.

People can help animals _____.

_____

More Vocabulary

 Look at the picture and read the word. Then read the sentences. Talk about the word with a partner. Write your own sentence.

destroyed

Wind **destroyed** the tree.

Which word means the same as *destroyed*?

played   hurt   helped

What does wind destroy?

Wind destroys _____

_____ .

struggle

The baby **struggles** to walk.

What words mean *struggle*?

moves fast   tries hard   slows down

What is something you struggle to do?

I struggle when I _____

_____ .

Words and Phrases: Suffix -er

The suffix -er means "a person who does something."

Who is someone who teaches?

A **teach**er teaches.

Who works on the street?

The **work**ers work on the street.

Talk with a partner. Look at the pictures. Read the sentences. Add the suffix -er to the underlined word. Write the new word.

Ann <u>trains</u> the dog. Ann is a
_____.

John <u>farms</u> his land. John is a
_____.

Text Evidence — Shared Read | Genre • Expository

1 Talk About It

Look at the photograph. Read the title. Discuss what you see. Use these words.

ocean   kids   rescue   sea   turtles

Write about what you see.

The text is about _____

_____

_____.

What do the kids rescue?

The kids rescue _____

_____.

Where does the sea turtle live?

The sea turtle lives _____

_____.

Take notes as you read the text.

KIDS to the Rescue!

Olivia and Carter are founders of One More Generation.

Essential Question

How can people help animals survive?

Read how two children helped sea turtles survive an oil spill.

It was a mess! Oil was everywhere. The oil floated on the water. It stuck to rocks and sand. The oil spill in the Gulf of Mexico made animals sick.

Two kids from Georgia watched **the news**. They saw pictures of sea turtles. The sea turtles were covered with oil. The kids watched the turtles **struggle** to move. The kids had to do something. The animals in the gulf needed help!

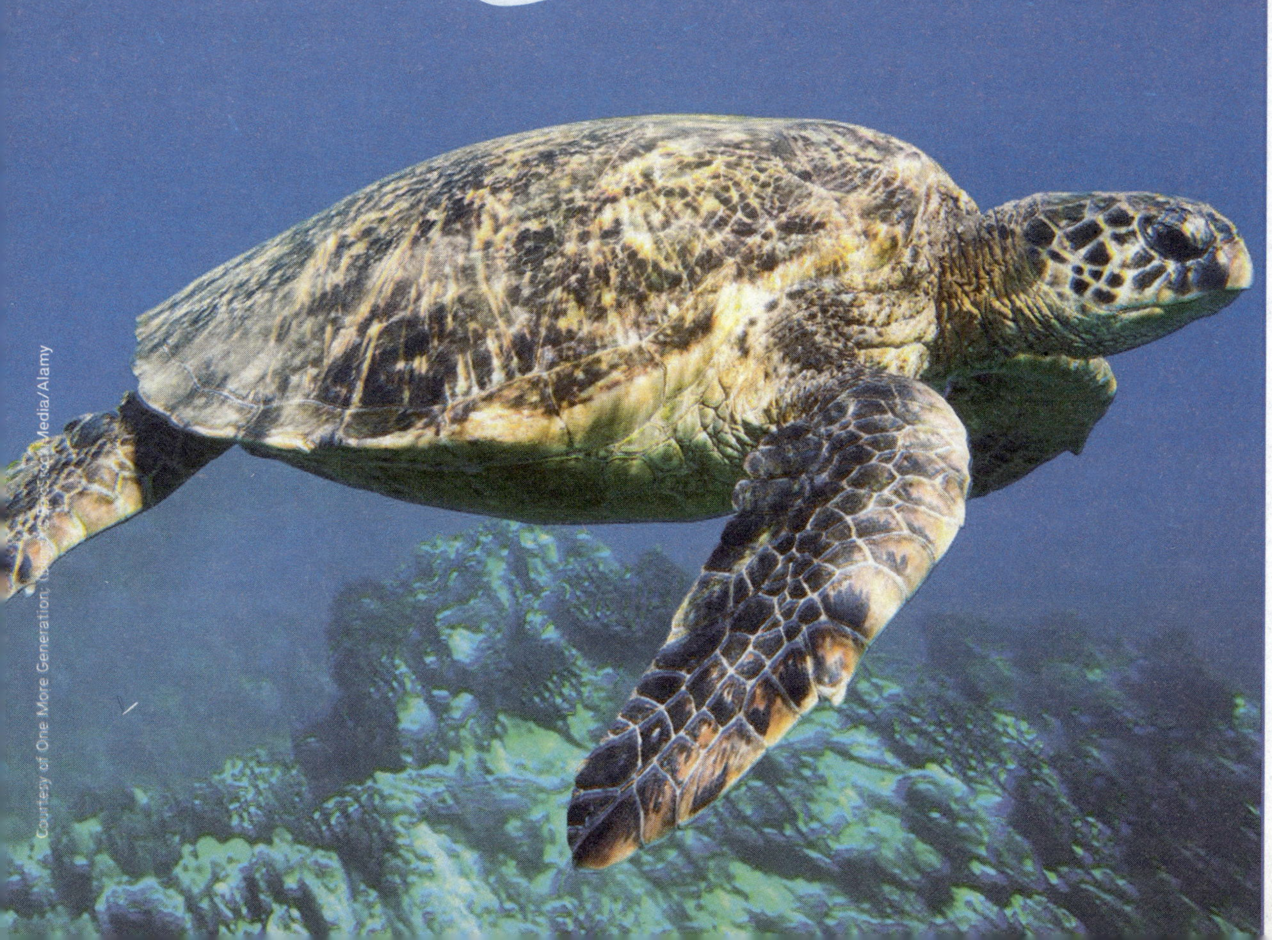

Text Evidence

❶ Comprehension
Author's Point of View

Look at the first sentence in the first paragraph. What does the author think about the spill?

The author thinks the spill was

_____.

❷ Specific Vocabulary

The news is a television program. It tells about events that are happening. What do the kids learn on the news? Underline the sentences that tell you.

❸ Talk About It

Why did animals in the gulf need help?

The animals needed help

because _____

_____.

51

Text Evidence

1. Sentence Structure

Look at the second sentence in the first paragraph. The pronoun *they* refers to more than one person. Circle the pronoun *they*. Who does *they* refer to?

_____

2. Specific Vocabulary

Reread the fourth sentence in the second paragraph. *Endangered* animals can die and become extinct. Underline the name of the endangered animal.

3. Talk About It

Why did Olivia and Carter name their group One More Generation?

The kids want animals to _____

_____.

Olivia and Carter to the Rescue!

Olivia and Carter Ries started a group to help animals. They named their group One More Generation. They want animals to be here in the future.

The oil spill got much larger. More and more animals got sick. The Kemp's ridley turtle got sick. They are **endangered**. There are only a few thousand Kemp's ridley turtles. The oil was close to their homes.

Olivia and Carter learned that oil hurts turtles.

Workers cleaned this female turtle. Now they are returning it to the gulf.

Oil Spoils Everything

Some turtles swam to Mexico. They wanted to lay eggs in Mexico. But the oil was harmful. It **destroyed** things the turtles need. Oil made it hard for the turtles to swim.

Turtles eat seaweed, jellyfish, and small sea animals. The oil spill **spoiled** their food. Without food, the turtles die.

Steven Senne/AP Images

Text Evidence

1 Sentence Structure ACT

Reread the first sentence in the second paragraph. Circle the commas. Underline the name of each food. Circle what eats these foods.

2 Specific Vocabulary ACT

Look at the word *spoiled* in the last paragraph. *Spoiled* means "harmed or ruined." What spoiled the turtles' food?

_____ spoiled their food.

3 Comprehension

How did the oil hurt the sea turtles?

The oil made it hard to _____

_____.

The oil made their food

_____.

53

Text Evidence

1 Sentence Structure

Reread the first sentence in the third paragraph. The word *as* connects two actions in the sentence. The actions happen at the same time. Underline the two actions.

2 Comprehension
Author's Point of View

Reread the third paragraph. What is the author's point of view about Olivia and Carter's plan? Underline the sentence that tells you.

3 Talk About It

What was the kids' plan for helping the turtles? Take notes. Then paraphrase the plan.

First, the kids _____.

Then they _____.

Next, they _____.

Saving the Sea Turtles

Olivia and Carter thought about the problem. The turtles needed help. First, the kids made a plan. Then they called a rescue group in New Orleans. The group needed materials. Next, the kids asked friends and relatives to help. Their friends and relatives donated materials.

Olivia and Carter collected materials. They traveled to New Orleans with their parents.

The kids watched as workers cleaned the sea turtles. Soon the turtles were spotless. Olivia and Carter's plan was a big success.

Going to New Orleans

Keeping Busy

Olivia and Carter work with other animal groups, too. They give talks at museums and schools. They ask leaders to help rescue animals.

Olivia and Carter are heroes to endangered animals. Many animals will survive with One More Generation's help.

Carter and his mom unpack supplies in New Orleans.

Ways to Help Animals!
- Protect animal homes.
- Pick up trash at parks.
- Keep water clean.
- Stop using plastic bags.

Make Connections

How did Olivia and Carter help the Kemp's ridley sea turtles? Describe the steps. ESSENTIAL QUESTION

What can you and your friends do to help animals? TEXT TO SELF

Text Evidence

❶ Specific Vocabulary

Look at the first sentence. The word *too* means "also." The words *too, to,* and *two* sound the same. Read the last paragraph. Circle the word that sounds the same as *too*.

❷ Comprehension

Author's Point of View

Reread the second paragraph. How does the author feel about Olivia and Carter? Underline the sentence that tells you.

❸ Talk About It

Describe some ways you can help animals. Look at the text for ideas.

I can help animals by _____

_____

_____.

55

Respond to the Text

 **Partner Discussion** Work with a partner. Read the questions about "Kids to the Rescue!" Show where you found text evidence. Write the page numbers. Then discuss what you learned.

What happened in the Gulf of Mexico?

An oil spill covered _____.

I read that the oil made animals _____.

In the text, the oil hurt turtles because _____
_____.

Text Evidence

Page(s): _____

Page(s): _____

Page(s): _____

How did Olivia and Carter help sea turtles survive?

Olivia and Carter wanted to help _____ because _____
_____.

I read that they started a group _____.

Olivia and Carter's plan was a success because _____.

Text Evidence

Page(s): _____

Page(s): _____

Page(s): _____

 **Group Discussion** Present your answers to the group. Cite text evidence for your ideas. Listen to and discuss the group's opinions.

Write Work with a partner. Look at your notes about "Kids to the Rescue!" Write your answer to the Essential Question. Use text evidence to support your answer. Use vocabulary words in your writing.

How did Olivia and Carter help sea turtles survive?

Sea turtles needed help because _____.

Olivia and Carter made a _____ and collected _____.

They went to _____.

Workers cleaned _____, and the plan was _____.

Share Writing Present your writing to the class. Discuss their opinions. Talk about their ideas. Explain why you agree or disagree with their ideas. You can say:

I agree with _____ because _____.

That's a good idea, but I think _____.

Write to Sources

pages 50–55

Take Notes About the Text I took notes on this idea web to answer the question: *How did the oil spill hurt the turtles?*

Rhett

- The oil covered the turtles.
- It was hard for the turtles to move.
- **The oil spill hurt the turtles.**
- Oil destroyed things the turtles need.
- The oil spoiled the turtles' food.

Write About the Text I used my idea web to write a paragraph about how the oil spill hurt the turtles.

Student Model: *Informative Text*

　　The oil spill hurt the turtles. First, the oil covered some of the turtles. Then it was hard for the turtles to move. The oil destroyed things the turtles needed. It spoiled their food. Some of the turtles died without food. The turtles needed help!

TALK ABOUT IT

Text Evidence
Draw a box around the second and third sentences. What words did Rhett use to show when these events happened?

Grammar
Circle the verb in the last sentence. What does the *-ed* at the end of the verb tell you?

Connect Ideas
Underline the two sentences about food. How can you combine the sentences?

Your Turn

Think about what Olivia and Carter do. Write a paragraph describing Olivia and Carter.

» Go Digital
Write your response online. Use your editing checklist.

TALK ABOUT IT

Weekly Concept Figure It Out

? Essential Question
How do people figure things out?

>> Go Digital

What is the boy doing? How can the family figure out where to go? Write the words in the web.

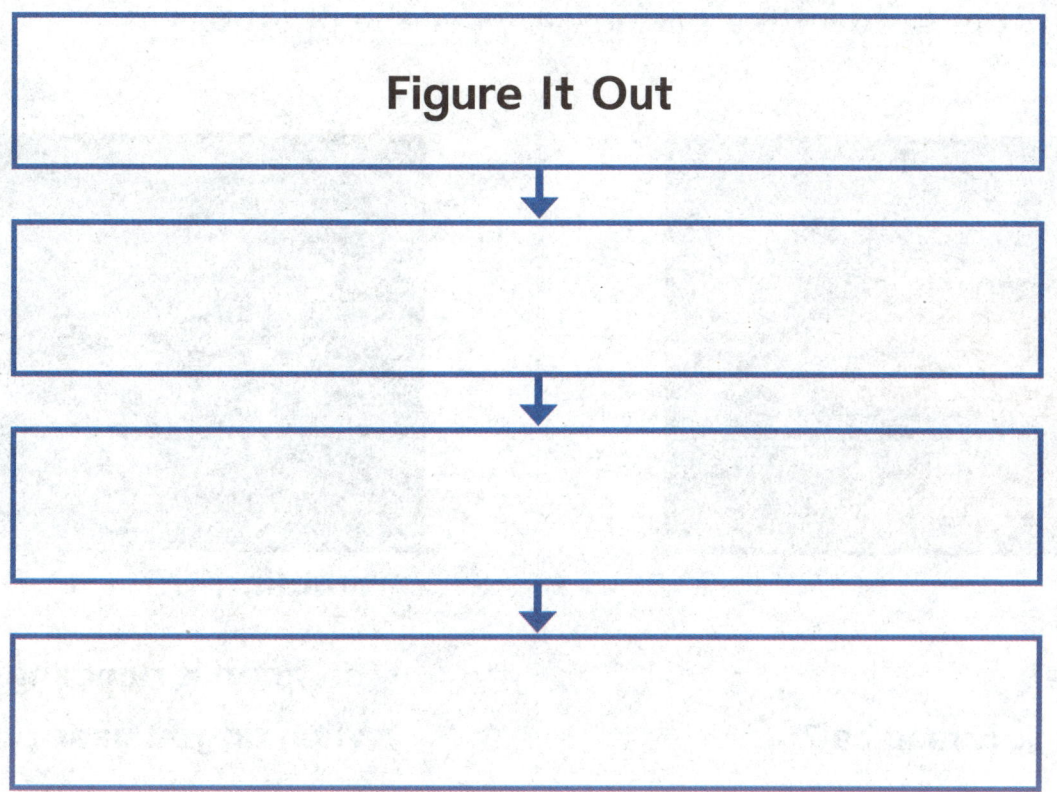

Figure It Out

Talk about how you figure out where to go. Use the words from the web. You can say:

First, I look at _____

I ask others _____.

I follow _____ along the way.

More Vocabulary

 Look at the picture. Read the word. Then read the sentences. Talk about the word with a partner. Answer the questions.

magical

The sky is **magical**.

What do you think is magical?

_____

_____

rumbling

The storm is **rumbling**.

When do you hear rumbling?

_____

_____

Poetry Terms

alliteration

Words with **alliteration** begin with the same sound.

Becky **b**ounces a **b**all.

simile

A **simile** compares two things. It uses the words *like* or *as*.

My **brother** sleeps <u>like</u> a **log**

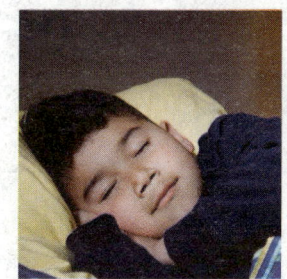 

rhyme

The words *bear* and *pear* **rhyme**. They end in the same sound.

I saw a **bear**
It ate a **pear.**

COLLABORATE

Work with a partner. Make up a rhyme. Use the words. Say the rhyme together.

ring   sing   king

We met a _____.

He had a _____.

He began to _____.

Text Evidence

Shared Read Genre • Poetry

1. **Talk About It**

   Look at the picture. Discuss who you see. What are they doing?

   I see _____ and _____.

   They are making _____.

2. **Comprehension**
   Point of View

   What is the boy's point of view about the empanadas? Underline the details that tell you.

3. **Literary Element**
   Rhyme

   Read the third and fourth lines. Which words rhyme? Circle the words.

Empanada Day

One bite of Abuelita's empanadas
And my mouth purrs like a cat.
  "Teach me," I beg and bounce on my feet,
  "Teach me to make this magical treat."
Abuelita smiles,
  "Be an observer, watch and learn,
  Then you too can take a turn."

Essential Question

? How do people figure things out?

Read a poem about a way to figure things out.

64

She sets before me a ball of dough,
Round and golden as the sun.
My eyes wide as saucers, I watch and follow,
   Press circles flat as pancakes,
      Spoon on apple slices and nose-tickling spices,
   Seal it all in, a half-moon envelope of **bliss**.
Together we write down every step
As the empanadas bake and crisp in the oven,
My stomach **rumbling** like a hungry bear.
               Ah, empanada day!
                              — George Santiago

Make Connections

? What is a way to figure something out? Talk about what happens in the poem. ESSENTIAL QUESTION

When have you figured something out? TEXT TO SELF

Text Evidence

1 **Literary Element**
Simile

Read the first two lines. What is the ball of dough like? Underline the words that tell you.

2 **Specific Vocabulary**

Look at the sixth line. The word *bliss* means "a very happy feeling." Why does the boy feel bliss? Draw a box around the words that tell you.

3 **Talk About It**

Reread the simile in the last line. What does the simile describe? How does this simile help you understand the boy?

The boy feels _____

_____.

65

Respond to the Text

 **Partner Discussion** Work with a partner. Read the questions about "Empanada Day." Show where you found text evidence. Write the page numbers. Then discuss what you learned.

What are Abuelita and her grandson doing?

Today is _____.

The boy begs Abuelita _____.

Abuelita tells him _____
_____.

Text Evidence

Page(s): _____

Page(s): _____

Page(s): _____

How does the boy learn to make empanadas?

The boy watches Abuelita _____.

Then he watches her _____ and _____.

Together Abuelita and the boy _____.

Text Evidence

Page(s): _____

Page(s): _____

Page(s): _____

 **Group Discussion** Present your answers to the group. Cite text evidence for your ideas. Listen to and discuss the group's opinions.

I agree with you, but _____. I do not agree because _____.

Write Work with a partner. Look at your notes about "Empanada Day." Write your answer to the Essential Question. Use text evidence to support your answer. Use vocabulary words in your writing.

How does the boy learn how to make empanadas?

The boy begs Abuelita to _____.

Abuelita shows the boy how to _____

_____.

Then together Abuelita and the boy write down _____

_____.

Share Writing Present your writing to the class. Discuss their opinions. Talk about their ideas. Explain why you agree or disagree with their ideas. You can say:

I think your ideas are _____.

That's a good comment, but _____.

Write to Sources

Sophia

pages 64–65

Take Notes About the Text I took notes about the poem on this chart to answer the question: *Does the poet use alliteration?*

Name of Poem	Examples of Alliteration
"Empanada Day"	I <u>b</u>eg and <u>b</u>ounce on my feet Then you <u>t</u>oo can <u>t</u>ake a <u>t</u>urn

Write About the Text I used notes from my chart to write an informative paragraph.

Student Model: *Informative Text*

In the poem "Empanada Day," the poet uses alliteration. He writes, "Then you too can take a turn." The words "too," "take," and "turn" begin with the same sound. "Beg" starts with the letter *b*. "Bounce" starts with the letter *b*. These are examples of alliteration in the poem.

TALK ABOUT IT

Text Evidence
Circle words from the poem. Why does Sophia use these words?

Grammar
Underline the sentence Sophia writes at the end. How can you add the word *good* to describe the examples?

Condense Ideas
Draw a box around the sentences about words that start with the letter *b*. How can you use the word *and* to connect the ideas?

Your Turn

Does the poet use similes? Use text evidence in your writing.

>> Go Digital
Write your response online. Use your editing checklist.